# The Wisdom of
# Southern Football

# The Wisdom of Southern Football

## Common Sense and Uncommon Genius From 101 Gridiron Greats

*Compiled and Edited by Criswell Freeman*

WALNUT GROVE PRESS
P.O. Box 58128
Nashville, TN 37205
(615) 256-8584

ISBN 0-9640955-7-2

*The ideas expressed in this book are not, in all cases, exact quotations, as some have been edited for clarity and brevity. In all cases, the author has attempted to maintain the speaker's original intent. In some cases, material for this book was obtained from secondary sources, primarily print media. While every effort was made to ensure the accuracy of these sources, the accuracy cannot be guaranteed. For additions, deletions, corrections or clarifications in future editions of this text, please write WALNUT GROVE PRESS.*

WALNUT GROVE PRESS books are available at special discounts for sales in bulk purchases, fund-raising, or educational use. For information, contact WALNUT GROVE PRESS.

Printed in the United States of America

Book Design by Armour&Armour
Cover Design by Mary Mazer
Typesetting & Page Layout by Sue Gerdes
Edited by Alan Ross
2 3 4 5 6 7 8 9 10 •   96 97 98

ACKNOWLEDGMENTS
The author gratefully acknowledges the helpful support of Bud Ford, Johnny Franks, Mary Susan Freeman, Don Pippen, Margaret Queen, Langston Rogers, and all the writers who have chronicled Southern football.

To Bruce Spaulding

*A great friend to have when it's fourth and long*

# Contents

# Introduction

In Dixie, football is more than a sport — it's a way of life. For many fans, baseball and basketball are mere diversions to help pass time until the real action begins on the gridiron.

Southern football had humble beginnings in the late 1800's. Still recovering from the Civil War, Dixieland colleges were, for the most part, small and poor. Southern teams were no match for the powerhouses of the East. But gradually, a transformation occurred. First, private institutions such as the University of the South and Vanderbilt began to field winning squads. Then, as state schools began to grow and prosper, new traditions were established. Teams like Alabama, Tennessee, Georgia Tech, LSU and Auburn began to win games and fill stadiums. Traditionally black institutions such as Grambling, Florida A&M and Tennessee State also gained national recognition.

As Southern football grew in stature, so did team loyalty. For today's avid fan, school allegiance is a mark of identification and pride. Championships can lift the spirits of entire states, while defeats can cause regional melancholy. Such is the power of football in Dixie.

Over the last hundred years, the legends of Southern football have grown to mythical proportions. The great players and coaches live on through their words and their deeds. This book contains thoughts from 101 coaches, players, educators, and journalists. The advice herein applies not just to football — it also applies to life.

It has been said that football in the South is not just a sport, it's a religion. If so, this book is intended as a quick primer in the theology of the gridiron — Southern style.

# 1

## Southern Football

A hundred years ago, football in the South was little more than a curiosity. What a difference a century makes. Today, millions of Southerners join the weekly pilgrimage to their stadiums of choice. Tens of millions follow their favorite teams on television or radio. And names like Bryant, Jordan, Gaither and Neyland are spoken with a quiet reverence once reserved for the likes of Robert E. Lee and Stonewall Jackson.

How important is football to the South? Consider the words that follow.

In the East, college football
is a cultural exercise.
On the West coast, it is a
tourist attraction.
In the Midwest,
it is cannibalism.
But in the South, college
football is a religion,
and every Saturday
is holy day.

*Marino Casem*

Southerners are proud of their football heritage, their schools, and their teams. And they share a deep pride that goes with being from the South.

*George Mooney*

The collisions between players at various
times were about equal to the coming
together of two Spanish bulls.
This sight provoked much laughter.

*Lexington Daily Transcript, April 10, 1880*

On the occasion of the first Southern collegiate football game

The game of football is beginning to gain
a foothold in Knoxville.

*Knoxville Journal, November 20, 1891*

Atlanta will be the scene Saturday afternoon
of the first interstate intercollegiate
football game. Both teams have been
practicing for weeks.

*Atlanta Journal, February 17, 1892*

Alabama Polytechnic and Mechanical School at Auburn
Defeated the University of Georgia 10-0

Football is the game of the future in college life.

*Bill Little, 1892*

In six days, we defeated Texas, Texas A&M,
Tulane, LSU and Mississippi.
Our best asset was a marvelous spirit
generated by stamina and fiber.

*Henry G. Seibels, 1899*

Seibels was captain of the University of the South's squad
that travelled 2,000 miles to defeat five teams in six days.

Football season! Behold the time when the
football man girdeth his loin and doeth
great stunts where they that are in the
grandstand may marvel at him.

*Memphis Evening Scimitar  October 26, 1901*

# Southern football is not recognized or respected. Boys, here's your chance to change that forever.

*Wallace Wade*

Pre-game remarks prior to Alabama's 20 to 19
Rose Bowl victory over Washington in 1926

The greatest southern football victory
of all time was Alabama's Rose Bowl victory
over Washington. It gained permanent
esteem for southern football.

*George Leonard*

Football is a religion in the Southland, played
by the boys and relived daily by their families.

*Zipp Newman*

College football is a religion.
Its pilgrimages lead to Atlanta, New Orleans,
Oxford, Knoxville, and Clemson.

*Clyde Bolton*

I'm from Ohio, but if I'd known when I was two
what it was like down South, I would have
crawled here on hands and knees.

*Frank Sinkwich*

Down in the Southeast territory, college
football long ago became a geographical,
historical, or social event — sometimes all
three. The fans down there always have
somebody they especially
love to see whomped.

*John D. McCallum*

Football is the essence of America, but not
because of championships or titles. The drive
to compete — the guts to play — the will to
come from behind — the grace to walk off the
field a loser — that's the essence of football.

*Archie Manning*

Football is as American as Huckleberry Finn,
apple pie or E Pluribus Unum.

*Tonto Coleman*

Someone once said that
in the South,
there are three seasons:
football season,
recruiting season and
spring practice.

*Bob Bell*

# To Southerners, football is as essential as air conditioning.

*Dan Jenkins*

# 2

# Life Lessons

Robert Neyland was larger than life. After graduating from West Point and serving his nation with honors, he traveled to Knoxville in 1925 to become the ROTC instructor and football coach at the University of Tennessee. Emphasizing defense, this strict disciplinarian soon built a gridiron dynasty.

Each time his country put out the call, Bob Neyland followed an old Tennessee tradition by volunteering for duty. A close associate of Douglas MacArthur, Neyland served in Burma in 1934. He also served throughout World War II, finally earning the rank of general.

Neyland's teams won national championships and fashioned records that may never be broken. Among other feats, his Volunteers held opponents scoreless for 71 consecutive quarters. That's almost two complete seasons!

The General once observed that, "The lessons learned upon the football field are carried usefully on to the field of life." Words spoken by a man who knew a lot about football, but even more about life.

Don't run too fast through life.
You only have one.

*Bo Jackson*

Life is short, so don't waste any of it
carrying around a load of bitterness.
It only sours your life, and the world
won't pay any attention anyway.

*Pat Dye*

Face life now.

*Bobby Bowden*

Today, not tomorrow.

*Terry Bowden*

Yesterday is already a dream and tomorrow
is only a vision, but today well-lived makes
every yesterday a dream of happiness and
every tomorrow a vision of hope.

*General Robert Neyland's*
*Favorite Quotation from The Sanskrit*

Set your goals up there real high, and then
be serious about reaching them.

*Don Maynard*

Life is facing challenges, going through
them, and getting to the other side.

*D. D. Lewis*

Success is not a definition.
It is a constant, continuous journey.

*George H. Denny*

You can never tell when a break is coming
your way. That's why you've got
to go all out on every play.

*Shug Jordan*

You get out of life, and out of football,
exactly what you put into it. When a person
realizes this and acts accordingly,
he is sure to succeed.

*Bart Starr*

Don't be a spectator.
Don't let life pass you by.

*Lou Holtz*

Don't go to your grave with a life unused.

*Bobby Bowden*

Make something happen.

*Sign in Gene Stallings' Office at Texas A&M*

Don't live on the fading memories of your
forefathers. Go out and make your own
records, and leave some memories
for *others* to live by.

*Dan McGugin*

Learn from everyone, copy no one.

*Don Shula*

Believe in honest, positive dissent.

*Pat Dye*

If you don't like to worry, why do it?
It doesn't help your performance.

*Joe Namath*

Don't talk too much or too soon.

*Bear Bryant*

Praise loudly. Criticize softly.

*Lou Holtz*

If you don't have the best of everything,
make the best of everything you have.

*Erk Russell*

Excuses are no good. Your friends don't
need them, and your enemies
won't believe them.

*Jake Gaither*


In a crisis, don't hide behind anything or
anybody. They're going to find you anyway.

*Bear Bryant*


The man who complains about the way the
ball bounces is likely the one who dropped it.

*Lou Holtz*


Never confuse activities with results.

*Sign in Gene Stallings' Alabama Office*


In football, and in life,
you've got to keep proving yourself.

*Charlie McClendon*

# Don't burn your bridges at both ends.

*Bill Peterson*

Striving for happiness through achievement
should not be a goal. If it is,
you'll never reach it.

*Joe Gibbs*

When you make a mistake, admit it;
learn from it and don't repeat it.

*Bear Bryant*

If you're looking back, you're in trouble.

*Charlie McClendon*

In life, it's always fourth and one, and there
are those urging me to go for it.

*Joe Gibbs*

Always remember that
Goliath was a
40-point favorite over
Little David.

*Shug Jordan*

# Win without braggin'. Lose without acting the fool.

*Eddie Robinson*

# 3

# Gridiron Advice

Football is a game of sayings, slogans and mottoes. It is no coincidence that the greatest coaches have also been marvelous communicators. Heisman and McGugin began a tradition that was carried on by the likes of Bryant, Jordan, and Dietzel: each could deliver an important message in a memorable way.

# Gentlemen, it is better to have died as a small boy than to fumble this football.

*John Heisman*

The team that makes
the fewest mistakes wins.

*General Robert Neyland*

Never try to make friends
with your head coach.

*Terry Bradshaw*

My advice for defensive players:
Take the shortest route to the ball
and arrive in a bad humor.

*Bowden Wyatt*

Don't cuss. Don't argue with the officials.
And don't lose the game.

*John Heisman*

Don't think that the way you are today
is the way you'll always be.

*Vince Dooley*

Football changes and so do people.
The successful coach is the one who sets
the trend, not the one who follows it.

*Bear Bryant*

There is no single "best" way to do
something in football.

*Charlie McClendon*

The worst thing a coach can do is stand pat
and think the things that worked
yesterday will win tomorrow.
Intelligent changes must be made.

*Johnny Vaught*

I'm not too proud
to change. I like
to win too much.

*Bobby Bowden*

Football is a game of defense and field position.

*General Robert Neyland*

You've got to do everything well, but you've got to play defense first.

*Vince Dooley*

The passing team gets beat.

*Bobby Dodd*

Luck follows speed.

*Frank Broyles*

If you win, you win doing the things
you do best.

*Doug Dickey*

When you find your opponent's weak spot,
hammer it.

*John Heisman*

Minimize your mistakes, and magnify the
mistakes of your opponent.

*General Robert Neyland*

# When in doubt, punt!

*John Heisman*

# 4

# Character

Football is a game that requires courage, discipline and teamwork. Athletic skills, while helpful, never guarantee victory. To win consistently, coaches must instill values that will continue to serve their players long after the final snap is taken.

Ole Miss Chancellor Porter L. Fortune once observed, "Many coaches train boys to become football players. John Vaught trained boys to become men." Vaught had an enviable won-loss record, but his most significant legacy lives through the lives he touched. Vaught, like all great coaches, taught something much more important than football. He taught character.

Coaches should build men first
and football players second.

*Eddie Robinson*

Look for players with character and ability.
But remember, character comes first.

*Joe Gibbs*

You win with good people.
Character is just as important as ability.

*Don Shula*

I don't believe in miracles.
I believe in character.

*Pat Dye*

Discover the talent that God has given you.
Then, go out and make the most out of it.

*Steve Spurrier*

Don't wait to be a great man.
Be a great boy.

*Shug Jordan*

No matter what the other fellow does on
the field, don't let him lure you into a fight.
Uphold your dignity.

*Frank Thomas*

Self-discipline is an individual's greatest asset.

*Lou Holtz*

When it comes to celebrating,
act like you've been there before.

*Terry Bowden*

# Have a profound respect for discipline.

*Shug Jordan*

If you don't have discipline,
you can't have a successful program.

*Bear Bryant*

I'd rather have a self-made player than a
natural-made player. I'd rather have a guy
with less talent who works than one
with more talent who doesn't.

*Bum Phillips*

Wealth and status mean nothing
on the football field; effort and
unselfishness mean everything.

*Johnny Majors*

If you want to be first-class,
you've got to act first-class.

*Joe Namath*

What does it take to be
the best? Everything. And
everything is up to you.

*Emmitt Smith*

I am fundamentally sound in my business
and my philosophy because of what
I learned playing football.

*Jerry Jones*

Winning isn't getting ahead of others.
It's getting ahead of yourself.

*Roger Staubach*

If you believe in yourself and have dedication
and pride — and never quit, you'll be a winner.

*Bear Bryant*

For when that One Great Scorer comes to
mark against your name,
He writes — not that you won or lost —
but how you played the game.

*Grantland Rice*

# 5

# Attitude

Before becoming head coach at Georgia Southern, Erk Russell ran the defense at Georgia. He was also the team's amateur psychologist and resident expert on motivation. Erk once observed that, "The better you feel about yourself, the better the world looks."

Coach Russell was right.

In life, as in football, attitude is everything. If you're hoping to improve your record, consider the following words of wisdom. They're guaranteed to help you feel better about yourself *and* your world.

You live up — or down — to your expectations.

*Lou Holtz*

When you have confidence, you can have
a lot of fun. And when you're having fun,
you can do amazing things.

*Joe Namath*

Even if you're not starting, you have to believe
that you're as good as the guy
who's playing in front of you. I've been
second-string three times in my football
career, and each time I thought I was
better than the guy in front of me.

*Ken Stabler*

You're the only person who can decide where you want to go and how you're going to get there.

*Terry Bowden*

Mistakes take away your confidence, and
when you lose confidence, everything bad has
a compounding effect on you. When an athlete
is truly focusing, he or she doesn't hear
the negatives, and they have no effect.
That's control.

*Terry Bradshaw*

In turning a program around, the hardest thing
to do is convincing players that they can win.

*Bill Dooley*

I want players to think as positively as the
85-year-old man who married a 25-year-old
woman and bought a five-bedroom house
next to the elementary school.

*Charley Pell*

When it gets right down to the wood-chopping,
the key to winning is confidence.

*Darrell Royal*

If you let one game or
one play haunt you,
your mind's in
the wrong place.

*Ken Stabler*

If you're gonna be a winner, you got to have
a bad case of the wants.

*Erk Russell*

Never take your focus away
from the next game.

*Don Shula*

You can't be aggressive and
confused at the same time.

*Darrell Royal*

In the struggle between equal teams,
the difference is never physical
but invariably mental.

*General Robert Neyland*

Nothing has changed about what makes
a winner. A winner works his butt off
and is dependable. He's not always
the most talented, but he gives
everything on every play.

*Pat Dye*

I can reach a kid who doesn't have any
ability as long as he doesn't know it.

*Bear Bryant*

# It's how you show up at the showdown that counts.

*Homer Norton*

# 6

## Preparation

Big John Merritt, the legendary head coach at Tennessee State University, once observed, "Preparation is everything. When you take the field, you better know that the hay is in the barn." Big John was not alone in this philosophy. Winning coaches adhere to the Boy Scout motto "Be Prepared."

We can all take a page from Coach Merritt's playbook — we can prepare ourselves thoroughly for the tasks ahead. When we do, we'll improve our chances of success, and we'll make life a little more enjoyable. After all, it's a good feeling to know that the hay is in the barn.

Preparation is as necessary to successful
coaching as weather is to the weather man —
there must be some of it every day.

*Bobby Dodd*

What makes for success? Practice.
We scrimmage plays more than 100 times in
spring practice and another 100 times in the
fall. You don't develop good teeth eating
mush, and you don't learn good football
going through the motions.

*General Robert Neyland*

In the forties, we didn't practice like they do
today. We practiced four to six hours a day.
Everybody did.

*Frank Sinkwich*

Luck is what happens when
preparation meets opportunity.

*Darrell Royal*

Spectacular achievements are always preceded by unspectacular preparation.

*Roger Staubach*

A football team is like an army.
Your men must be in good physical condition.
They must have technical ability, and
they must have high morale.

*General Robert Neyland*

In a big game, you can't afford to be too high,
because if you start feeling like Hercules
out there, you'll make foolish mistakes.

*Terry Bradshaw*

Proper conditioning is that fleeting moment
between getting ready and going stale.

*Frank Thomas*

You have to be willing to out-condition
your opponents.

*Bear Bryant*

Practice doesn't make perfect.
Perfect practice makes perfect.

*Johnny Majors*

The greatest mistake is to continue
to practice a mistake.

*Bobby Bowden*

You play the way you practice. Practice the
right way, and you'll play the right way.

*Pop Warner*

There are two types of preparation —
physical and mental. You can't get by
with just one or the other.

*Ken Stabler*

You can have anything you want
if you're willing to pay the price.

*Eddie Robinson*

The fast life doesn't go well with football.
This is a violent sport and you have to
take care of your body to survive it.

*Deacon Jones*

To break training without permission
is an act of treason.

*John Heisman*

Sacrifice. Work. Self-discipline.
I teach these things, and my boys
don't forget them when they leave.

*Bear Bryant*

There are no office hours for champions.

*Paul Dietzel*

To be a winning team, you must be
a hungry team. So remember that
*every* football Saturday is the most
important date on the schedule.

*Johnny Vaught*

An angry football team is better than
a confident one.

*Pepper Rodgers*

Practice hard, but avoid the drudgery.
Make the practice routine fun.

*Bobby Dodd*

Keep the players high. Make practice
a pleasure, not a lark. Be a disciplinarian,
but not a slave driver. It's better to have
a short, full practice than a long lazy one.

*Frank Thomas*

First we will be best, then we will be first.

*Lou Holtz*

First, I prepare. Then I have faith.

*Joe Namath*

When you know what you're doing,
you don't get intercepted.

*Johnny Unitas*

# 7

# Tradition

Mississippi State and Texas coach Darrell Royal was asked to define tradition. He said, "When good things have happened over a period of years, and you expect good things to happen again — that's tradition."

Southern football is blessed with a tradition that leads to high expectations. Fans believe that good things should happen again and again. If victories are slow in coming, there's trouble for the home team.

But Southern rivalries, while intense, are not always bitter. Bob Fulton was the voice of the South Carolina Gamecocks for 43 years. When he announced his final game at Carolina's big rival, Clemson, he was presented with a plaque. How did the Tiger fans respond? During the ceremony, 85,000 die-hard Clemson supporters rose as one to give the Carolina announcer a long, heartfelt standing ovation. That sort of sportsmanship exemplifies the best in Southern football: the love for one's school and the respect for one's opponents.

The true football fan pays no attention to time
or mileage when there is a big game to see.

*John Heisman*

Tradition is a rich asset for any team.
Tradition and success are traveling companions.

*Wallace Wade*

After so many years at a school,
you become a member of the football family.

*Bob Fulton*

In Baton Rouge, it's not a law to love LSU,
but the city fathers could probably get
one passed if they needed to.

*Charlie McClendon*

In Baton Rogue, the focal point of everything
is Tiger football.

*Jim Corbett*

The wild excitement inside Tiger Stadium
is shattering. It's like an electric wire
running from the stands to the field.

*Charlie McClendon*

I'd rather face the lions in the Coliseum than
the Tigers in Baton Rogue

*Bobby Dodd*

*Tradition*

I believe in Auburn ... and love it.

*Dr. George Petrie*

There's a closeness that all Auburn people feel.
It's the War Eagle Spirit.

*Shug Jordan*

The secret of Auburn's success? The fans.
The Auburn people are the secret
to the greatness of Auburn.

*Pat Dye*

When we play Alabama, the coaches
don't need to prepare pep talks.

*Shug Jordan*

Tennessee sophomores don't deserve
citizenship papers until they have survived
an Alabama game.

*General Robert Neyland*

Any Florida boy who is worth a cuss
better come to A&M.

*Jake Gaither*

When you hear forty-six thousand Rebels
screaming for your blood — and meaning
it — it can be a little eerie.

*Vince Dooley*

I don't care where a man comes from or
how he spells his name. All I ask is that he
be loyal to Georgia, proud of that jersey,
and try like the devil to win.

*Wally Butts*

I was looking for a name for our defense.
A supporter said, "Why don't you use
Junkyard Dogs?" I didn't think it was original
enough, but I couldn't think of anything better, so we went with it.

*Erk Russell*

## Tradition

Folks in South Carolina are not just great fans,
they're great people.

*Bob Fulton*


At Georgia Southern, we don't cheat.
That costs money, and we don't have it.

*Erk Russell*


My sales pitch to recruits was simple:
At Arkansas, we have great fans,
great tradition, and few distractions.

*Frank Broyles*


I'd rather be on probation
than get beat by Furman.

*Clemson Bumper Sticker*


I had a lot of offers to go to other schools,
but I turned them all down. Clemson was
the only place I could bum chewing tobacco
from the professors.

*Frank Howard*

It's the Alabama spirit — that indescribable something which made the efforts of a small team bring seemingly impossible results.

*D. V. Graves*

Alabama, thy name is courage — unyielding valor in all its splendor! Flow on Crimson. Thou hast brought honors aplenty to Dixieland.

*Zipp Newman, January 1, 1927*

Alabama people sure love their football.

*Homer Smith*

The definition of an atheist in Alabama is someone who doesn't believe in Bear Bryant.

*Wally Butts*

Southern football fans are knowledgeable,
fair — and loud.

*George Mooney*

Here at Vanderbilt, we have some scars,
but we also have stars!

*Dan McGugin*

People who haven't been to Knoxville on
a football Saturday can't understand the
experience. It's excitement beyond description.

*Bob Bell*

The best teams have their fans
in the stands an hour before kickoff.

*Brad Scott*

Mama called.

*Bear Bryant*
His explanation for leaving a championship team at Texas A&M
to return to his struggling alma mater, Alabama

# 8

# Winning & Losing

Football games are denominated in wins and losses. Win enough games, and they name the stadium for you. Lose too many, and they name your replacement.

Before playing Alabama in 1969, Shug Jordan borrowed much of his pre-game speech from the Book of Ecclesiastes:

"Men, there is a time for everything. A time to live and a time to die; a time to love and a time to hate; a time for peace and a time for war. And gentlemen, there's a time to beat Alabama. That time is now!"

Though gaining no medals for originality, Shug's pep talk achieved the desired results — Auburn won the game. Jordan eventually went down as one of the most beloved coaches in history — and yes, they did name the stadium for him.

$B$e a gracious winner
and an understanding loser.

*Joe Namath*

$L$earn to lose grudgingly, but gracefully.
Learn to win with humility.

*Tonto Coleman*

$W$inning is not final.

*Don Shula*

$I$ expect peak performance from myself,
my staff, and my players.
Sometimes you lose anyway.

*Joe Gibbs*

The only way I know to keep football fun
is to win. There is no laughter in losing.

*Darrell Royal*

When you win, there's glory enough
for everybody. When you lose,
there's glory for none.

*Bear Bryant*

To win it all, a team has to be obsessive
about the fundamentals and the little things.

*Joe Gibbs*

It's not the number of plays you have,
but how you execute them.

*General Robert Neyland*

Close only counts
in horseshoes and hand grenades.

*Frank Howard*

We came to win, not to tie.
If I had it do over a hundred times,
I would do the same thing.

*Paul Dietzel*

After a two-point conversion failed resulting in a 14-13 loss to
Tennessee. The loss ended LSU's 19-game winning streak.

When you're number one,
you don't play for the tie.

*Bear Bryant*

I consider a tie a loss.

*Johnny Vaught*

A tie is like kissing your sister.

*Abe Martin*

They say a tie is like kissing your sister.
I guess it's still better than
kissing your brother.

*Lou Holtz*

Public relations is great, but there's
no public relations like winning.

*Tom Landry*

The heck with statistics. Just win.

*Terry Bradshaw*

Winning isn't everything.
It's the only thing.

*Red Sanders*

Winning isn't the only thing,
but it beats whatever comes in second.

*Sign in Bear Bryant's office*

I don't believe in a jinx or a hex. Winning
depends on how well you block and tackle.

*Shug Jordan*

Almost all games are lost by the losers,
not won by the winners.

*General Robert Neyland*

You play 50 or 60 plays a game
for the privilege of making three or four
that make the difference.

*Gene Stallings*

You don't think about the close games
you win — it's the close ones
you lose that you think about.

*Frank Broyles*

When they look back at that 9-1 season,
they don't ask who the nine were.

*General Robert Neyland*

Expect to lose sometimes, but a loss can be
a stepping stone to victory if
it's utilized in the right way.

*Jake Gaither*


In losing, we learn a lot of football.

*Bill Alexander*


Sure losses hurt,
but football isn't life and death.

*Bobby Bowden*

# When you win, nothing hurts.

*Joe Namath*

# 9

# Leadership

In 1860, Emerson wrote, "There are men, who, by their sympathetic attractions, carry nations with them, and lead the activities of the human race." Thirty years later, football was introduced to Dixieland, and a new Southern leader emerged: the football coach. Initially, most of the great coaches were Northerners, but soon, Dixie began producing field generals of heroic proportion.

If you hope to change your world, consider the following words. They appear courtesy of men who, by their sympathetic attractions, led their teams to victory.

Nobody wants to follow somebody who doesn't know where he's going.

*Joe Namath*

Leadership, like coaching, is fighting
for the hearts and souls of men and
getting them to believe in you.

*Eddie Robinson*

Coaches should be masterful, commanding,
even dictatorial. A coach has no time
to say "please" or "mister."
Occasionally, he must be severe.

*John Heisman*

Lots of leaders want to be popular. I never
cared about that. I want to be respected.

*Don Shula*

I just organize. Give me credit
for selecting good assistants.

*Jake Gaither*

Organize. Deputize. And supervise.

*Biff Jones*

I don't have any ideas; my coaches have them.
I just pass the ideas on and
referee the arguments.

*Bear Bryant*

I don't hire anybody not brighter than I am.
If they're not smarter than me,
I don't need them.

*Bear Bryant*

All of Bear's boys are good motivators.

*Bob Fulton*

Every time a player goes out there,
at least 20 people have some amount of
influence on him. His mother has more
influence than anyone. I know because
I played, and I loved my mama.

*Bear Bryant*

If anything goes bad, I did it. If anything goes
semi-good, we did it. If anything goes real
good, you did it. That's all it takes to get
people to win football games.

*Bear Bryant*

One of the greatest things Coach Bryant
used to do was *pass along the credit.*

*Gene Stallings*

Our boys *have* to be motivated.
They don't have much opportunity. We teach
them that they can't afford to waste it.

*John Merritt*

When you lose, you doubt yourself and
your plans. Losing creates doubt just
like winning creates momentum.

*Danny Ford*

It's a lot easier to keep motivated
when you're winning.

*Gordon Wood*

It is important to keep the squad eternally
aware of the very nature of football
so that they are not dismayed
when things are going wrong.

*General Robert Neyland*

You can motivate by fear.
And you can motivate by reward.
But those methods are only temporary.
The only lasting motivation is self-motivation.

*Homer Smith*


I don't ask players to "Win one for the Gipper."
I ask them to win one for themselves.

*Tommy Prothro*


Motivation is simple.
You eliminate those who aren't motivated.

*Lou Holtz*

# Leadership must be demonstrated, not announced.

*Fran Tarkenton*

# 10

# Adversity

No coach, no player, no team can avoid adversity. Football is a game of injuries, penalties, turnovers and bad bounces. Each weekend, as many teams lose as win. Whether it's high school, college or the professional ranks, adversity always lurks near the gridiron, stalking the ill-prepared or the unlucky.

In 1963, Tulane's Tommy O'Brien spoke for unfortunates everywhere when he lamented his squad's 0-10 record: "Last season was a tough way to break in a new coach — especially when that coach happened to be me!"

If you're facing tough times, don't despair and don't give up. And by all means, keep your sense of humor. Like Coach O'Brien, you're going to need it.

In life, you'll have your back up against
the wall many times. You might
as well get used to it.

*Bear Bryant*

The sun doesn't shine on the same dog
every day.

*Steve Sloan*

Lord, don't remove my stumbling blocks —
just give me strength.

*Earl Campbell*

Turn a setback into a comeback.

*Billy Brewer*

If I'm a good football coach, it's because of
my mistakes. I try to learn from them.

*Steve Spurrier*

Difficulties in life are intended
to make us better, not bitter.

*Dan Reeves*

Growing up, we didn't have money or status.
You had to work and hustle. Hustling made
you resourceful and work made you hard,
and I was doing both by the time I was 11.

*Joe Namath*

You can be anything you want —
if you're willing to pay the price.

*Eddie Robinson*

You never know how a horse will pull
until you hook him to a heavy load.

*Bear Bryant*

You never know what a football player
is made of until he plays Alabama.

*General Robert Neyland*

Defeat is a bitter pill. But if you take it as
a lesson, defeat may not be as bad as it seems.

*Homer Norton*

Football is a lot like engineering.
If you work long and hard enough, you can
come up with the answer to the problem.

*Charlie Shira*

To appreciate the good things in life,
you've got to have seen some hard times.

*Earl Campbell*

It's no disgrace to get knocked down —
so long as you get back up.

*Darrell Royal*

The first time you quit, it's hard.
The second time, it gets easier. The third
time, you don't even have to think about it.

*Bear Bryant*

The lessons in my life have come from
failures, my own shortcomings, naiveté and
buying into some of the biggest myths
modern society has to sell.

*Joe Gibbs*

You may fail a thousand times, but success
may be hiding behind the next step.
You never know how close the prize is
unless you continue.

*Bob Tyler*

No matter how bad things seem,
never give up.

*Chucky Mullins*

Don't give up at half time. Concentrate on
winning the second half.

*Bear Bryant*

# 11

## Teamwork

Football games are won and lost by teams, not individuals. Victory requires the concerted efforts of players, coaches, trainers, administrators and fans. Even the brightest star is limited by the play of his teammates.

Gridiron success requires hard work and teamwork. That's football. And that's life.

That's the thing about sports. Once people can play together, they see they can live together.

*Eddie Robinson*

Football is not an "I" game. It's a "we" game.

*Pat Dye*

One guy can't do it by himself and it's
a matter of recognizing this and giving
others their share of the credit.

*Archie Manning*

You can accomplish anything as long as
you don't care who gets the credit.

*Blanton Collier*

There are two kinds of discipline:
self-discipline and team discipline.
You need both.

*Vince Dooley*

Football is an honest game. It's true to life.
It's a game about sharing.
Football is a team game. So is life.

*Joe Namath*

Football is like the game of life.
　　You're forced to help your fellow man.
　　You cannot be your best unless your
　　　teammates are doing their job.

*Joe Namath*

To old football players,
　　teammates neither die nor ever fade away.

*Nash Buckingham*

You cannot really be good without seniors
　　　who are big winners.

*Darrell Royal*

To be good, a team must have good seniors.

*Johnny Majors*

What makes a championship team?
Leadership, dedication, and teamwork.

*Matty Bell*

Discipline, with team togetherness,
wins football games.

*Johnny Vaught*

The first thing any coaching staff must do
is weed out selfishness. No program
can be successful with players who
put themselves ahead of the team.

*Johnny Majors*

One man doesn't make a team. It takes 11.

*Bear Bryant*

You'll never know how
much God means to you,
Till tragedy hits and
friends come through.

*Chucky Mullins*

# 12

## Coaching Advice

In the 1903 Clemson yearbook, John Heisman wrote, "It is hardly an exaggeration to say that the scientific development of the game of football is only beginning to be realized." How prophetic were those words. Today, the game has reached a level of sophistication that would have amazed even a visionary like Heisman.

Despite great technical advancements, the most important principles of coaching haven't changed much in the last hundred years. The game evolves, but certain truths remain.

If you were to ask me if football is a coach's
game, I'd have to say it is. And always was.

*Bear Bryant*

A coach has to fit into the mold
of the school, the community, and the state.

*Bob Fulton*

The coach is the team, and the team
is the coach. You reflect each other.

*Tommy Prothro*

The worst mistake any coach can make
is not being himself.

*Charlie McClendon*

The head coach must remain a little aloof
from the players and, to a certain extent,
from the coaches.

*General Robert Neyland*

Coach a boy as if he were your own son.
*Eddie Robinson*

Either love your players
            or get out of coaching.
*Bobby Dodd*

Never try to fool a player.
            You can't kid a kid.
*Darrell Royal*

Urge church attendance.
*Bobby Dodd*

It's bad coaching to blame your boys
            for losing a game, even if it's true.
*Jake Gaither*

No athletic program can ever be better
than its recruiting.

*Frank Broyles*

The worst mistake a coach can make is
to get caught without material.

*Red Sanders*

Recruiting is and will remain an inexact
and highly speculative science.

*Frank Broyles*

I'm known as a recruiter. Well, you've got
to have chicken to make chicken salad.

*Bear Bryant*

I don't have uniforms that fit
men under 250 pounds.

*Eddie Robinson*

A coach is like an auto mechanic who has all the parts of a car laid out. If there's a piece missing, the thing won't work. You've got to find that piece.

*Bobby Bowden*

My coaching philosophy? Determine your players' talents and give them every weapon to get the most from those talents.

*Don Shula*

The secret to winning is constant, consistent management.

*Tom Landry*

Bear Bryant's Three Rules for coaching:
1. Surround yourself with people who can't live without football.
2. Recognize winners.
   They come in all forms.
3. Have a plan for everything.

You never get comfortable in this game.

*Dan Reeves*

If you're a football coach, criticism comes
with the territory. If it tears you up,
you better get into another profession.

*Pat Dye*

To err is human, to forgive is divine.
But to forgive a football coach is unheard of.

*Vince Dooley*

Coaching is nothing more than eliminating
mistakes before you get fired.

*Lou Holtz*

There's only two kinds of coaches:
them that's been fired and
them that's about to be fired.

*Bum Phillips*

The first thing a football coach needs when
he's starting out is a wife who's willing
to put up with a whole lot of neglect.
The second thing is a five-year contract.

*Bear Bryant*

As a coach, the alumni you have to worry
about are the ones you never see.

*Wally Butts*

The alumni are starting to grumble, and
I'm the one starting it.

*Bear Bryant*

Remarks after a close loss.

I retired for health reasons.
The alumni got sick of me.

*Frank Howard*

When they run you out of town,
make it look like you're leading the parade.

*Bill Battle*

Borrow from other coaches.
Pick and choose the things that work for you.
But you've got to coach to suit
your own personality.

*Bill Dooley*

You have to listen to your assistant coaches.
They're young and aggressive and always
looking for a way to improve.

*Bobby Dodd*

No head coach can be better than his staff.
Show me a winning team, and I'll show you
a good group of assistant coaches.

*Johnny Majors*

You must learn how to hold a team together.
You lift some men up, calm others down,
until finally they've got one heartbeat.
Then, you've got yourself a team.

*Bear Bryant*


Never leave the field with a boy feeling
you're mad at him. You can chew him out,
but then pat him on the shoulder.

*Jake Gaither*


How do you win?
By getting average players to play good
and good players to play great.
That's how you win.

*Bum Phillips*


Keep rules to a minimum
and enforce the ones you have.

*Vince Dooley*

No coach has ever won a game by what he knows; it's what his players know that counts.

*Bear Bryant*

Win or lose, one thing is always
the same — you can't relax.

*Bill Dooley*

Football coaching is hard work.
It drains heavily on the physical, particularly on the nerves. I believe that one should cease this arduous service while still in good health.

*Dan McGugin*

I just send the kids out there on the field
and tell 'em to have fun.

*Abe Martin*

There ought to be a special place in heaven for coaches' wives.

*Bear Bryant*

I want my boys <u>ag</u>-ile, <u>mo</u>-bile, and <u>hos</u>-tile.

*Jake Gaither*

# 13

## Game Day

How big is game day in the South? In 1934 Huey Long bullied the Illinois Central Railroad into offering discounted fares so that LSU fans could attend the Vanderbilt game in Nashville. LSU won 29-0 with Senator Long delivering the halftime speech.

A year later, during his halftime sermon, SMU coach Matty Bell warned his boys that, "You've got 30 minutes to play and a lifetime to think about it."

In '36 a strapping Arkansas lad named Paul Bryant suited up for the Alabama Crimson Tide despite having a broken leg. Young Bear took it all in stride, commenting, "It's only a little bone."

Neither broken bones nor railroad companies can interfere with game day in Dixieland. Players and fans intuitively know that Coach Bell was right: the game is all too brief, but the memories remain for a lifetime.

The game is the star of the show. My only job is to help the audience enjoy it.

*Keith Jackson*

You are about to be put through an ordeal
which will show the stuff that's in you.
What a glorious chance you have!

*Dan McGugin*

To his undefeated Vanderbilt squad in 1921

I don't care how much talent a team has —
if the boys don't think tough,
practice tough, and live tough,
how can they play tough on Saturday?

*Bear Bryant*

I want to coach a team that opponents
don't look forward to playing.

*Danny Ford*

My special trouble is that I am now coaching
one of the teams I'd most want to play.

*Steve Sloan*
*Vanderbilt, 1973*

How you fight is how you will be remembered.

*Dan McGugin*

Football is as primitive as hand-to-hand combat. No quarter is asked or given.

*Mike Donahue*

Sometimes, you have to bleed for the cause.

*Erk Russell*

You may be scared to death, but don't admit it, even to yourself.

*Terry Bradshaw*

All I ask is that you give everything you've got on every play. That's not asking very much.

*Shug Jordan*

At Auburn, practice is hell. But when you line up across from the big, fast, smart, angry boys from Florida, and Georgia, and Alabama, where there is no quality of mercy on the ground and no place to hide, you'll know why practice is hell at Auburn.

*Pat Dye*

Play for your own self-respect and the respect of your teammates.

*Dan McGugin*

Winning isn't imperative, but getting tougher in the fourth quarter is.

*Bear Bryant*

Hit 'em hard and carry 'em to the ground.
It reduces their enthusiasm.

*Dan McGugin*

You can last a little longer if you know when
to hit the big licks and when to avoid them.

*Jim Taylor*

I grew up pickin' cotton on my daddy's farm.
To me, football is like a day off.

*Lee Roy Jordan*

If you've got the game under control,
don't do anything to interrupt the flow.

*Joe Namath*

On game day, I want my boys happy.

*Jake Gaither*

On game day, I'm as
nervous as a pig
in a packing plant.

*Darrell Royal*

# 14

# The Coaches

In 1903, John Heisman observed that, "Successful coaches are few and far between, and it is small wonder they command salaries practically without limit." If Heisman was impressed with turn-of-the-century wages, he would be flabbergasted by the pay scale of today's top coaches. Many things have changed since Heisman's day, but one thing remains the same: Great coaches — like the ones on the following pages — are *still* few and far between.

## The Coaches

Dan McGugin mixed a lot of fun
with his football, an ingredient
the game needs more of today.

*Fred Russell*

I bought a cemetery plot overlooking
Memorial Stadium. That's where I'll spend all
eternity, listening to the cheers for my Tigers.

*Frank Howard*

I drive a Cadillac, not because I like it,
but because boys who live on dirt floors
are bound to be impressed.

*John Merritt*

I've seen that glint in Eddie Robinson's eye.
He's got that old feeling that you get
when you're about to kill a gnat
with a sledgehammer.

*Marino Casem*

I never won a single game
in my life.
The players did.

*Eddie Robinson*

# In Dodd We Trust.

*Slogan about Tennessee All-American and*
*Georgia Tech coach Bobby Dodd*

I'd rather have a good high school coaching
job than a lousy pro coaching job.

*Bum Phillips*

I had to leave Texas. As long as
Gordon Wood was there, I could never
be the best coach in the state.

*Bear Bryant*

Referring To Wood, the legendary Texas high school coach

Hopefully, the future of our nation will fall
into the hands of young men like those
coached by Brownwood's Gordon Wood.

*Lyndon B. Johnson*

Paul (Bear) Bryant, the "great rehabilitator"
at Maryland, Kentucky, and most recently at
Texas A&M, now faces his stiffest challenge in
14 years as a head coach. He inherits an Alabama squad that has won only four of 30
games in the past three years.

*Sports Illustrated, September 22, 1958*

Alabama fans love Bryant
and tolerate the rest of us.

*Gene Stallings*

Bear Bryant could take his'n and beat your'n
or he could take your'n and beat his'n.

*Bum Phillips*

The first "bear" in Alabama football wasn't Bear Bryant. It was Wallace Wade, Bama's coach in the Twenties. The players called him bear because he was mean and tough — but they never called him bear to his face.

*Hoyt "Wu" Winslett*

Boys, I'd like to introduce you to Coach Wallace Wade. He's the man responsible for the great tradition of Alabama football.

*Bear Bryant*

Introducing Wade at a practice in 1980

Erk Russell.
What a coach!
What an unforgettable
character! What a man!

*Vince Dooley*

# 15

## The Players

The South's first collegiate football game took place in 1880. Since then, countless young men have suited up to play. Every Southern village has its high school squad, complete with mascot, team colors, and bygone heroes. A young man with potential will find every opportunity to sharpen his gridiron skills, whether he's from the big city of Atlanta, the Florida Everglades, the Mississippi Delta or the hills of Tennessee.

Certain players have magic. They rise above the crowd, making a place for themselves in the history books. Their extraordinary achievements have become part of the fabric of Southern football.

Bear Bryant once observed that, "Football is a game of studs, and if you want to win you better have some." The following passages recognize a few of these gridiron greats.

The best all-purpose back of his era was
Charley Trippi of Georgia. In his prime, he
removed the ceiling of what one man
could mean to a football team.

*Fred Russell*

Outside the Louisiana Purchase in 1803,
many Cajuns consider Billy Cannon's run
the greatest event in state history.

*John Vaught*

Describing Cannon's 1959 Halloween-night jaunt
that defeated Ole Miss 7-3

The best Southeastern Conference player
in the last 11 years ... BILLY CANNON.

*Athlon Southeastern Football, 1969*

Archie Manning was Mississippi's
combination Sir Lancelot and Superman.

*Fred Russell*

Joe Namath could have been a superstar in
basketball, baseball, or any other sport.
He was that good.

*Lee Roy Jordan*

George Rogers was the nicest guy you
would ever want to meet. He also happened
to be the best player we ever had.

*Bob Fulton*

I wouldn't say Earl Campbell was in a class
by himself, but I can tell you one thing:
It sure don't take long to call the roll.

*Bum Phillips*

Eldridge Dickey was so valuable to my team
that I never let him out of my sight. Heck,
that boy ate Christmas dinner with me!

*John Merritt*

I've seen a lot of great college offensive linemen. The greatest was John Hannah.

*Bob Bell*

Tucker Frederickson was the most complete football player I've seen in the 40 years I've been connected with the game.

*Shug Jordan*

The Lord has a lot to say about football. He gave me a good body, speed and quickness. When you got it, you got it.

*John "Shipwreck" Kelly*

They asked me about Johnny Mack Brown becoming a movie star. I told 'em the boy had to make a living somehow.

*Wallace Wade*

I guess I'm just too full of Bama.

*Tommy Lewis*

Explaining why he came off the sidelines to tackle Dickie Moegle in the 1954 Cotton Bowl

Deep inside, we're still the boys of autumn, that magic time of the year that once swept us on to America's fields.

*Archie Manning*

Coach, don't feel sorry for me.
I've had a wonderful 29 years.

*Pat Trammell*

This is the saddest day of my life.

*Bear Bryant*

Upon hearing of Pat Trammell's death

# 16

## Observations on Kickers, Turnovers, and Other Facts of Life

We conclude with a potpourri of wisdom. Enjoy.

Money is no big deal. What I value is
my family and what I got from
my momma and daddy.

*Eddie Robinson*

When we have a good team, I know it's
because we have boys that come from
good mommas and pappas.

*Bear Bryant*

If you burn your neighbor's house down,
it doesn't make your house look any better.

*Lou Holtz*

It is better to have faith in a cause that will
ultimately succeed than to succeed
in a cause that will ultimately fail.

*Bobby Bowden*

The price of victory is high,
but so are the rewards.

*Bear Bryant*

When I talk to kids about football,
I talk to them about having fun.

*Archie Manning*

Poise means never fighting yourself.

*Bob Tyler*

I can't believe God put us
on this earth to be ordinary.

*Lou Holtz*

# Kindness is the universal language that all people understand.

*Jake Gaither*

If you think you're lucky,
you are.

*Bobby Dodd*

You've got to be in a position for luck
    to happen. Luck doesn't go around
        looking for a stumblebum.

*Darrell Royal*

Sure, luck means a lot in football.
    Not having a good quarterback is bad luck.

*Don Shula*

When all is said and done,
        more is said than done.

*Lou Holtz*

Age has nothing to do with it.
    You can be out of touch at any age.

*Bear Bryant*

In the football business, if you're
        standing still, you're losing ground.

*Doug Dickey*

The athletic field is very democratic.
Each person is judged by personal merit
rather than personal wealth or prestige.

*Paul Dietzel*

Treat turnovers like a copperhead
in the bedclothes; avoid them at all costs.

*Darrell Royal*

Kids in Texas are not impressed
by each other's press clippings.
They know each other too well.

*Jess Neely*

Everybody at LSU wants another great
team like '58. The only trouble is that our
schedule is so tough, we could have
a great year and never know it.

*Charlie McClendon*

To be a great halfback, you need to be as
quick as a hiccup, and you better run like
you just stole a government mule.

*John Merritt*

Any athlete with pride wants
to compete against the best.

*Lance Alworth*

Nobody ever got backslapped
into winning anything.

*Wallace Wade*

To defeat a weak opponent is not
the problem: The problem is to win when
he is as good or better than you.

*General Robert Neyland*

Bad teams are creative.
They always find a new way to lose.

*Archie Manning*

I love the thrill of getting off a pass
just before getting smashed.

*George Blanda*

Happiness is being able to lay your head
on the pillow at night and sleep.

*Herschel Walker*

I never get tired of running.
The ball ain't that heavy.

*Herschel Walker*

Let sleeping bags lie.

*Bill Peterson*

Kickers are like golfers:
90 percent confidence, 9 percent technique
and 1 percent ability.

*Jimmy Johnson*

My golf game reminds me of Woody Hayes.
Three yards and a cloud of dust.

*Bill Dooley*

# God doesn't want your ability — He wants your availability.

*Bobby Bowden*

The drama of sport is a big part of the drama of life, and the scope of this drama is endless.

*Grantland Rice*

# Sources

# Sources

All sources are coaches or players
unless otherwise noted.
Southern school affiliations
appear in parentheses.

Eddie Robinson (Grambling): 34, 44, 63, 85, 93, 98, 105, 106, 125, 138

Pepper Rodgers (Georgia Tech, Memphian): 65

Darrell Royal (Texas, Mississippi State): 54, 56, 60, 67, 77, 95, 100, 105, 122, 142, 143

Erk Russell (Georgia Defensive Coordinator, 1964-1980; Georgia Southern): 29, 51, 56, 71, 72, 118

Fred Russell (Journalist, Author): 124, 132

Red Sanders (Vanderbilt): 79, 106

Brad Scott (Florida State, South Carolina): 74

Henry G. Seibels (University of the South): 19

Charlie Shira (Mississippi State): 94

Don Shula (Miami Dolphins): 28, 45, 56, 76, 85, 107, 142

Frank Sinkwich (First Southern Heisman Trophy Winner, Georgia): 21, 60

Steve Sloan (Alabama, Vanderbilt, Texas Tech, Mississippi): 92, 117

Emmitt Smith (Florida, Dallas Cowboys): 49

Homer Smith (Scholar, Alabama Offensive Coordinator, Author): 73, 89

Steve Spurrier (Florida): 45, 93

Ken Stabler (Alabama): 52, 55, 63

Gene Stallings (Alabama): 28, 30, 80, 87, 128

Bart Starr (Alabama): 27
Roger Staubach: (Dallas Cowboys): 50, 61
Jim Taylor (LSU): 121
Fran Tarkenton (Georgia): 90
Frank Thomas (Alabama, UT-Chattanooga): 46, 62, 65
Dr. Pat Trammell (Alabama, 1940-1968): 136
Bob Tyler (Mississippi State): 96, 139
Johnny Unitas (Louisville): 66
Johnny Vaught (Mississippi, Texas Christian): 38, 65, 78, 101, 132
Wallace Wade (Alabama, Duke): 20, 68, 134, 144
Herschel Walker (Georgia): 145, 146
Pop Warner (Georgia): 63
Gordon Wood (Legendary High School Coach; Brownwood, Texas): 88
Hoyt "Wu" Winslett (Alabama): 129
Bowden Wyatt (Tennessee): 37

# Notes

*Notes*

*Notes*

*Notes*

*Notes*

# About the Author

Criswell Freeman is a Doctor of Clinical Psychology living in Nashville, Tennessee. He is the author of *When Life Throws You a Curveball, Hit It* and *The Wisdom Series* from WALNUT GROVE PRESS. He is also a published country music songwriter.

Dr. Freeman received his undergraduate degree from Vanderbilt University in 1976. He is a lifelong fan of Southern Football.

# About Wisdom Books

Wisdom Books chronicle memorable quotations in an easy-to-read style. Written by Criswell Freeman, this series provides inspiring, thoughtful and humorous messages from entertainers, athletes, scientists, politicians, clerics, writers and renegades. Each title focuses on a particular region or special interest.

Combining his passion for quotations with extensive training in psychology, Dr. Freeman revisits timeless themes such as perseverance, courage, love, forgiveness and faith.

"Quotations help us remember the simple yet profound truths that give life perspective and meaning," notes Freeman. "When it comes to life's most important lessons, we can all use gentle reminders."

# The Wisdom Series
*by Dr. Criswell Freeman*

## Wisdom Made In America
ISBN 1-887655-07-7

## The Book of Southern Wisdom
ISBN 0-9640955-3-X

## The Book of Country Music Wisdom
ISBN 0-9640955-1-3

## The Golfer's Book of Wisdom
ISBN 0-9640955-6-4

## The Wisdom of Southern Football
ISBN 0-9640955-7-2

## The Book of Texas Wisdom
ISBN 0-9640955-8-0

## The Book of Florida Wisdom
ISBN 0-9640955-9-9

## The Book of Stock Car Wisdom
ISBN 1-887655-12-3

## The Wisdom of Old-Time Baseball
ISBN 1-887655-08-5

Wisdom Books are available through
booksellers everywhere. For information about
a retailer near you, call 1-800-256-8584.